Horror Coloring Book For Adults

WEREWOLF MONSTER FARM

Fantasy Art Coloring Book For Stress Relief

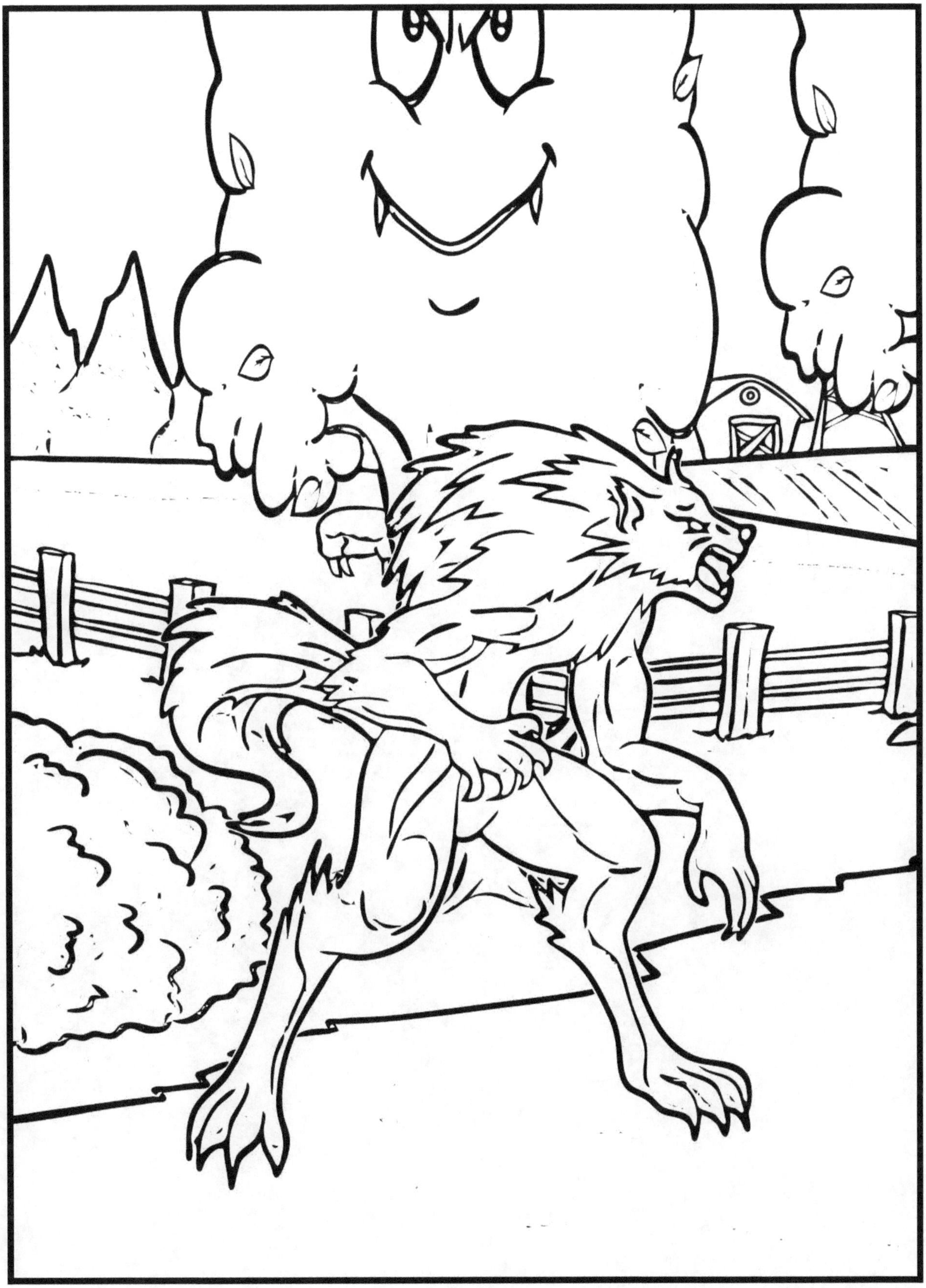

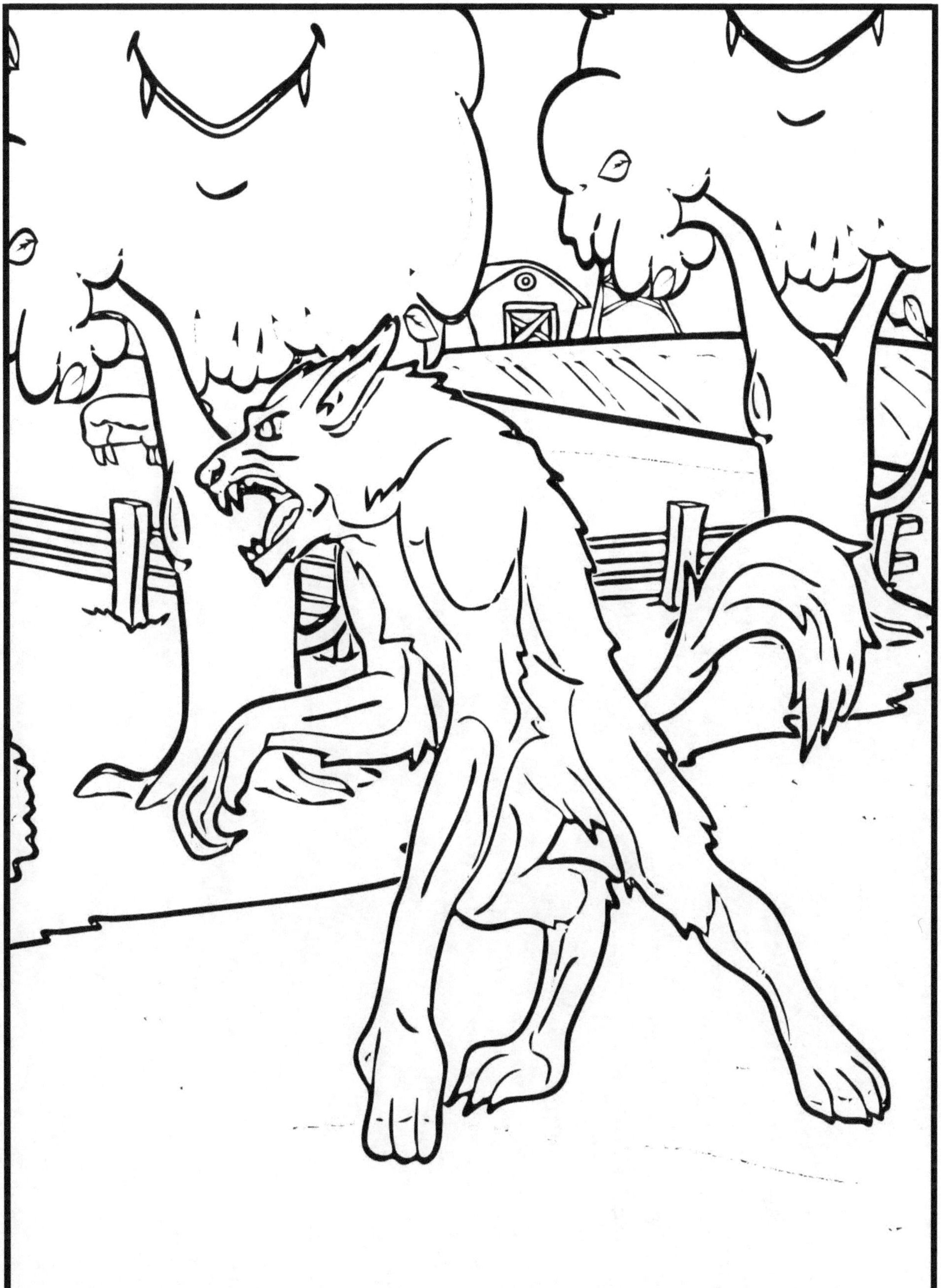

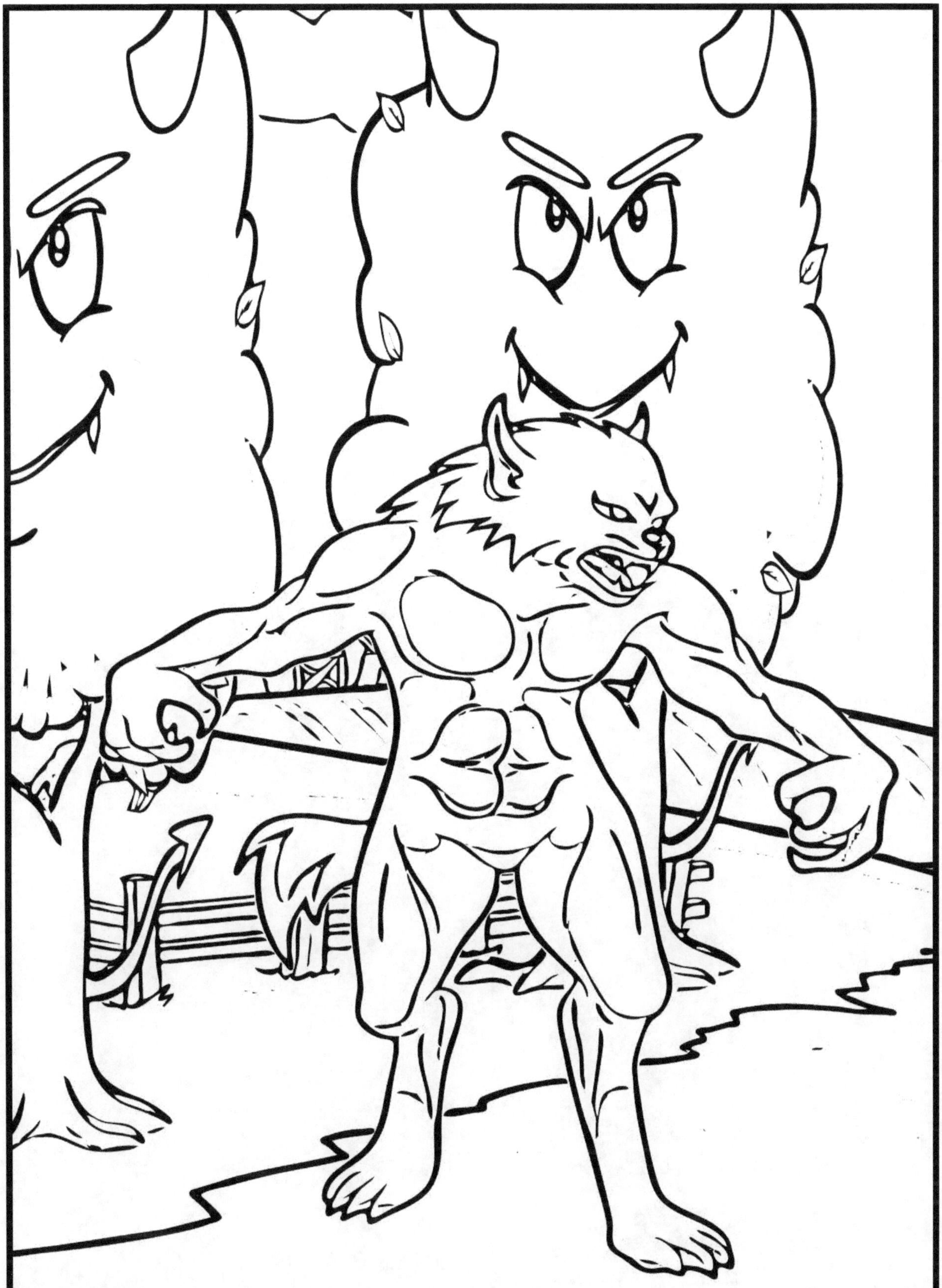

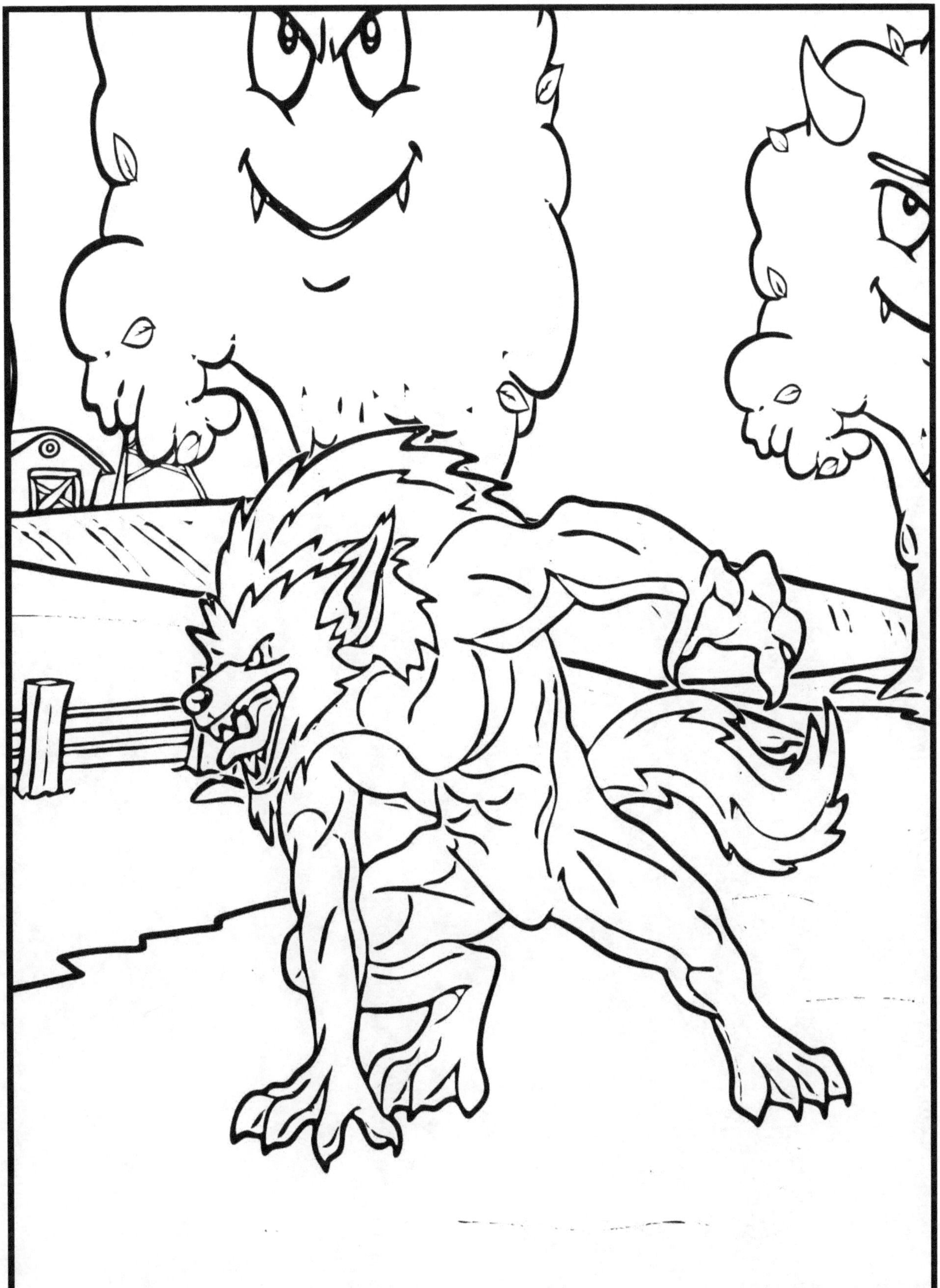

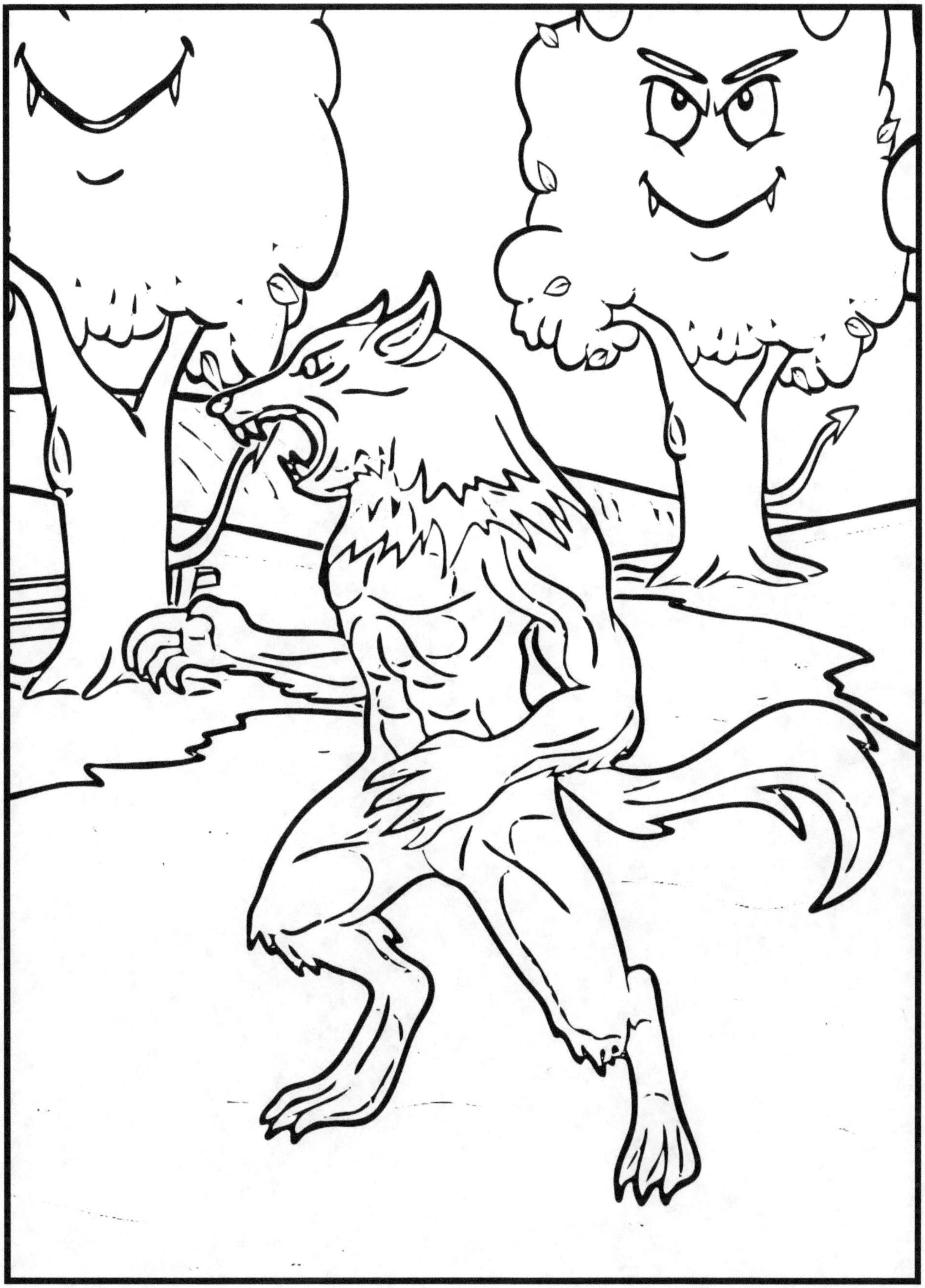

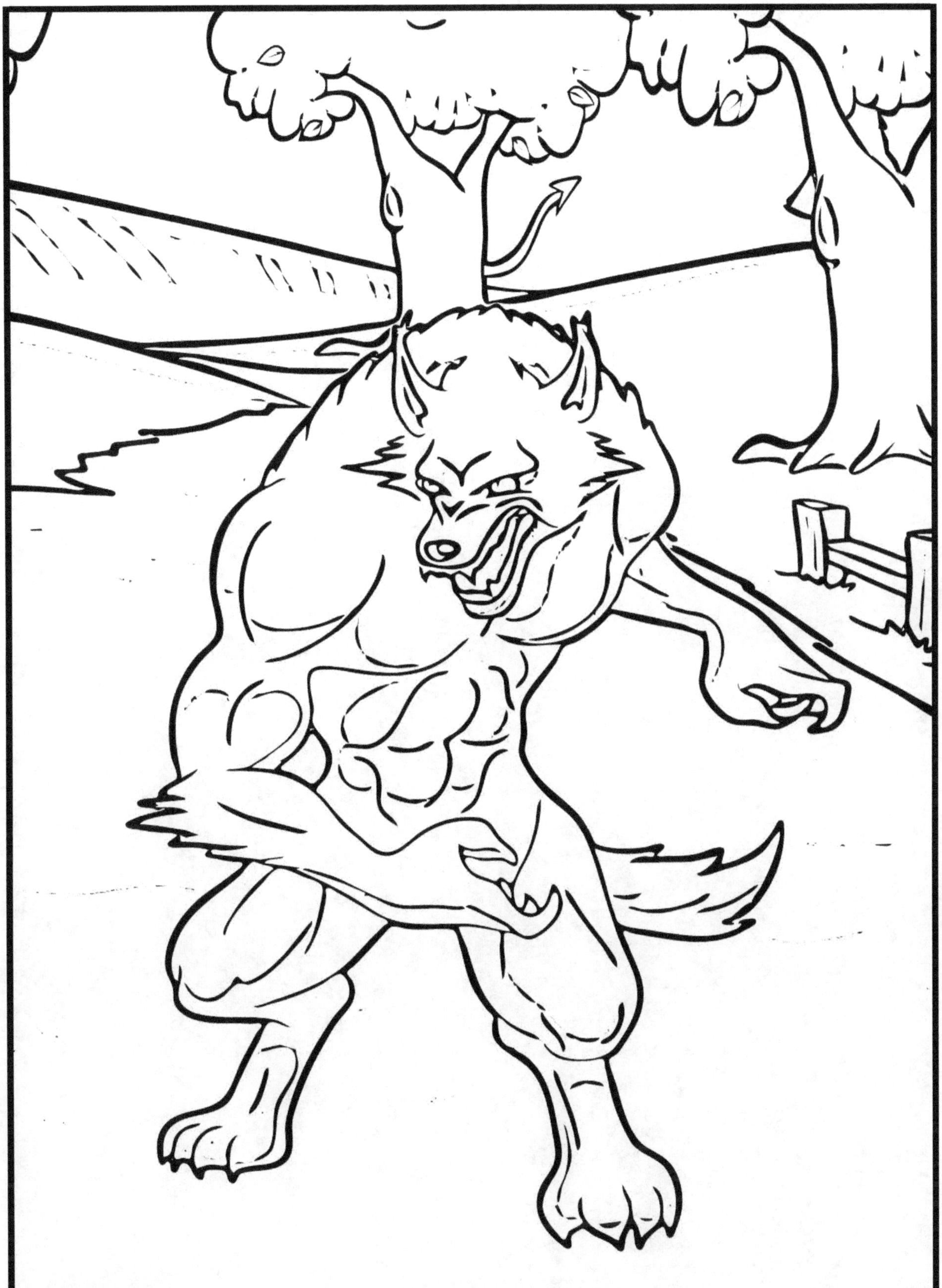

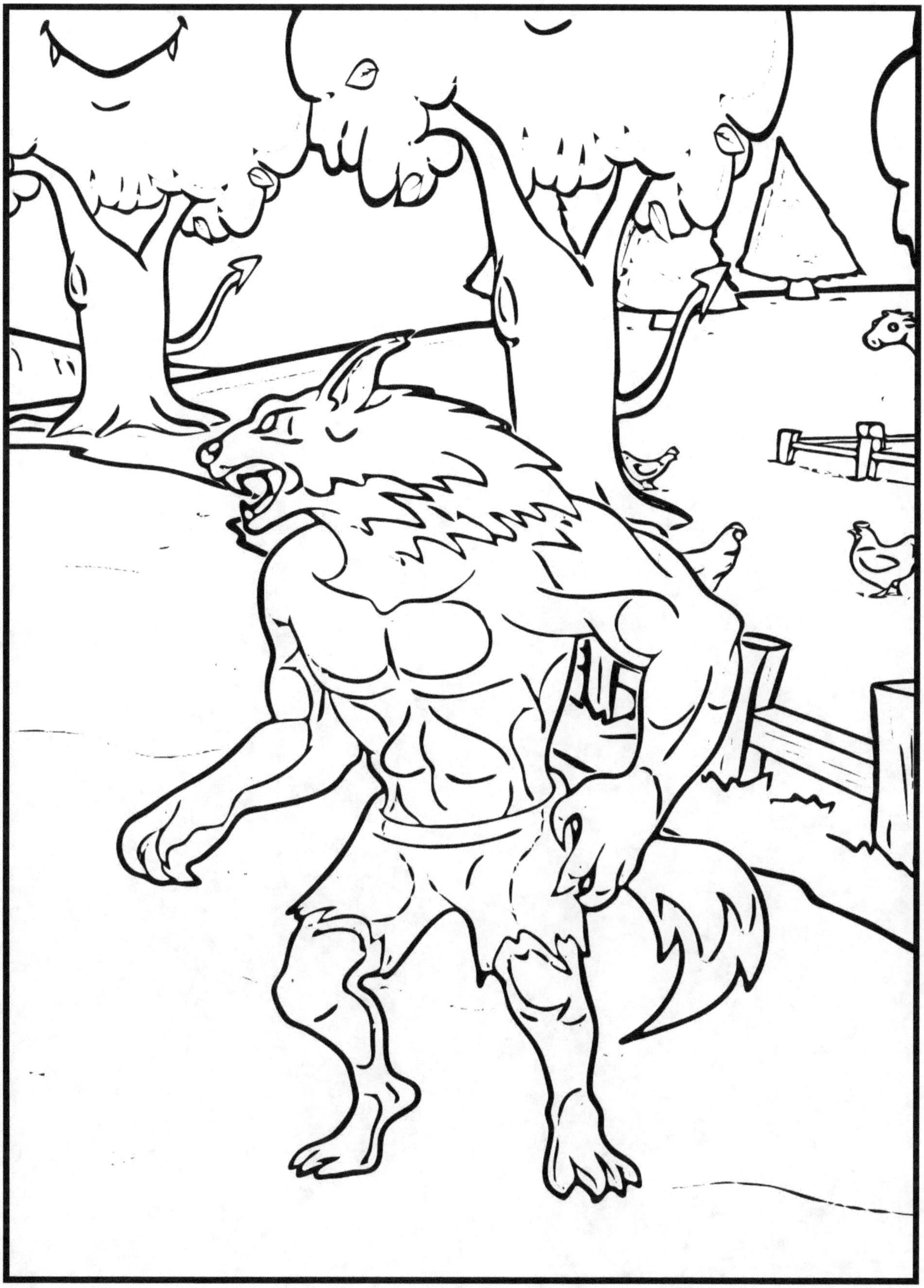

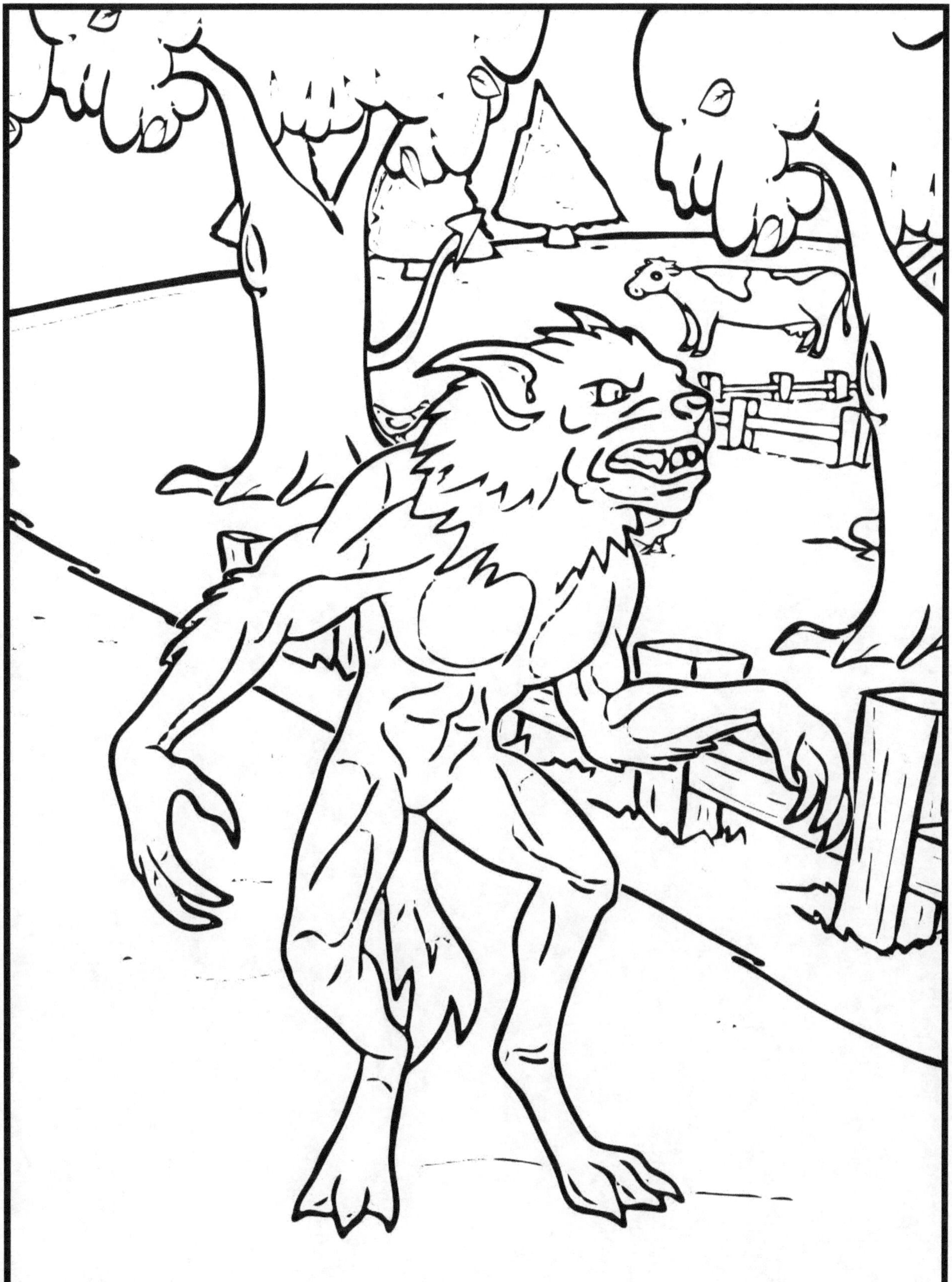

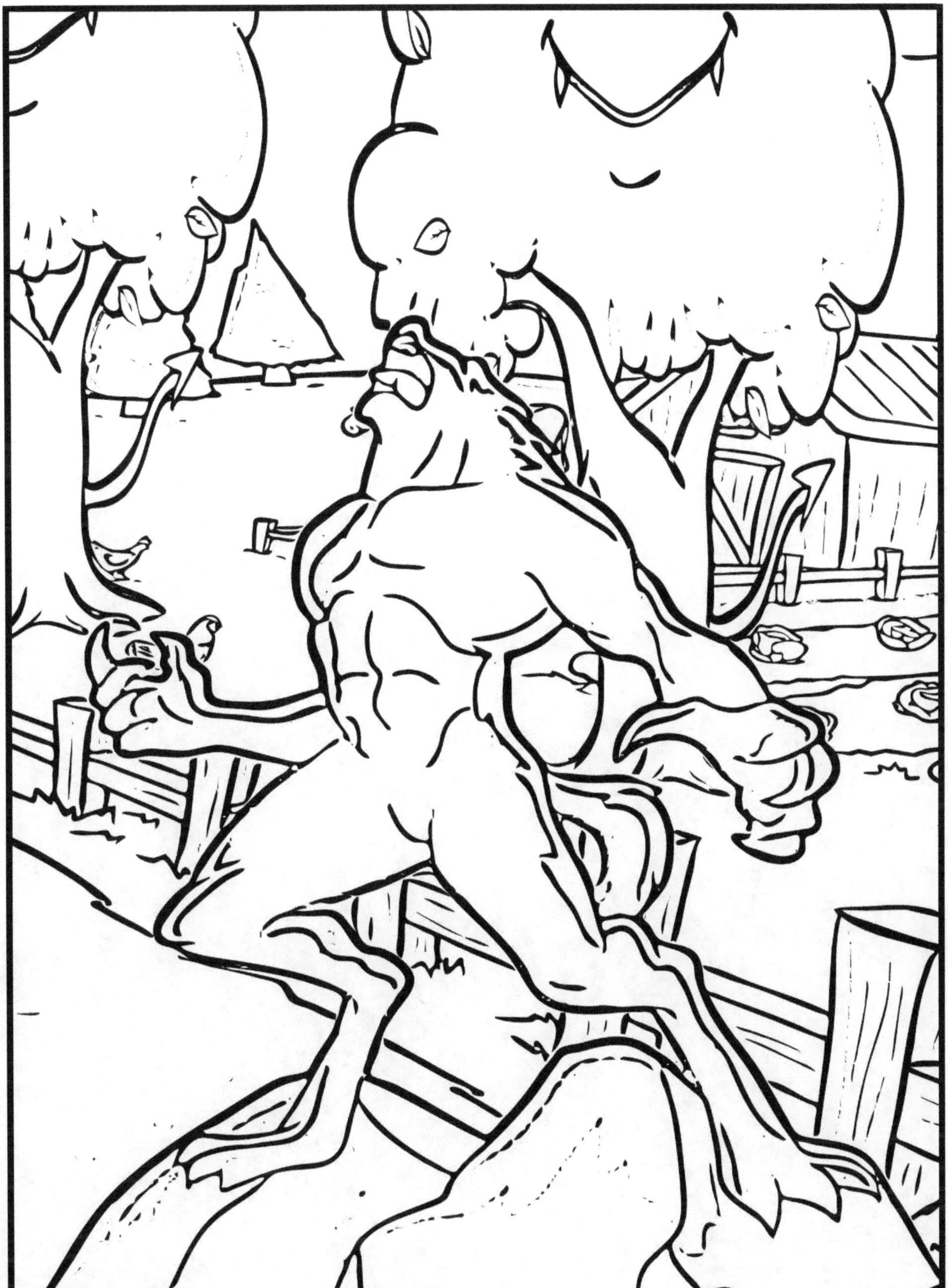

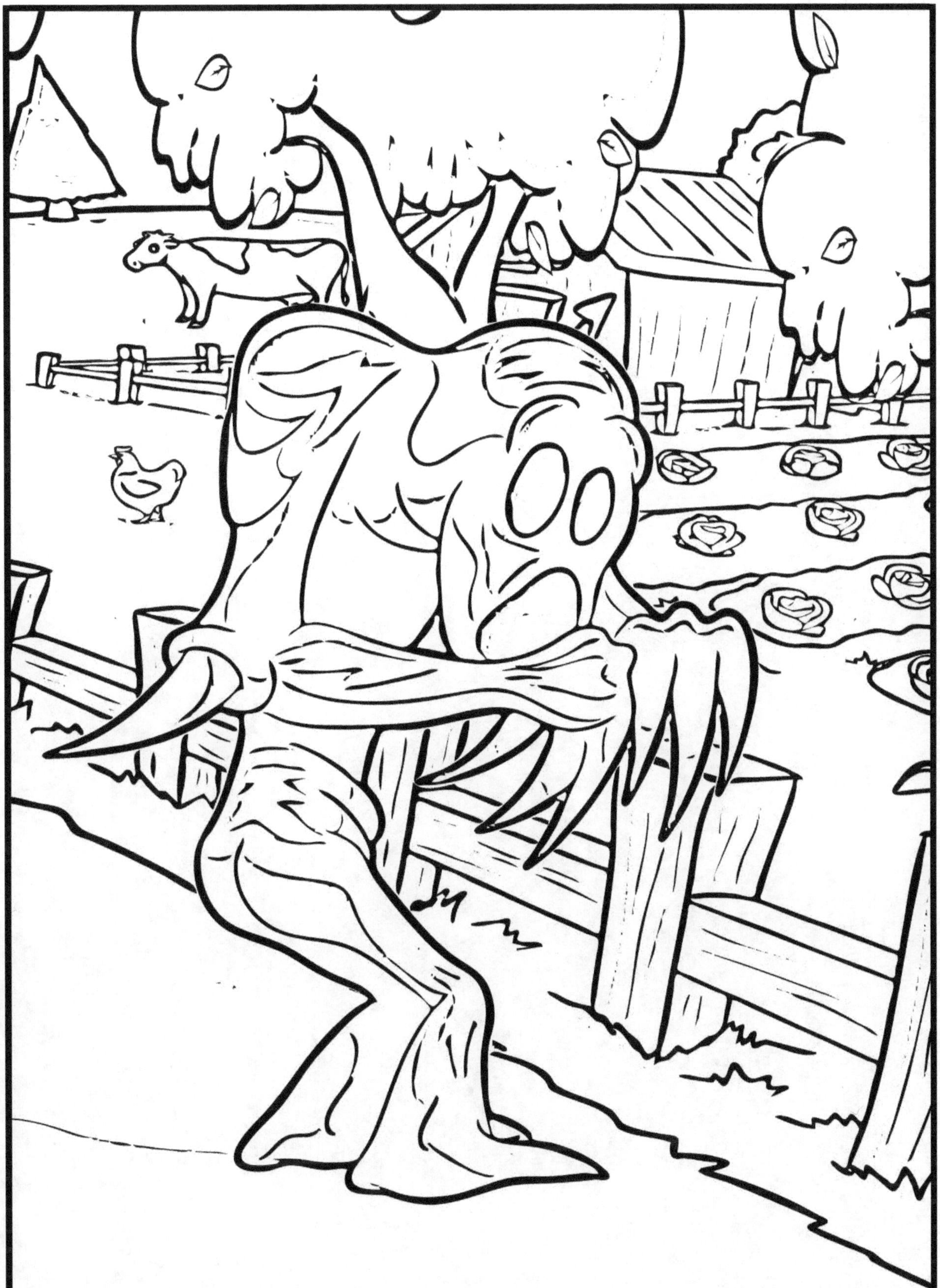

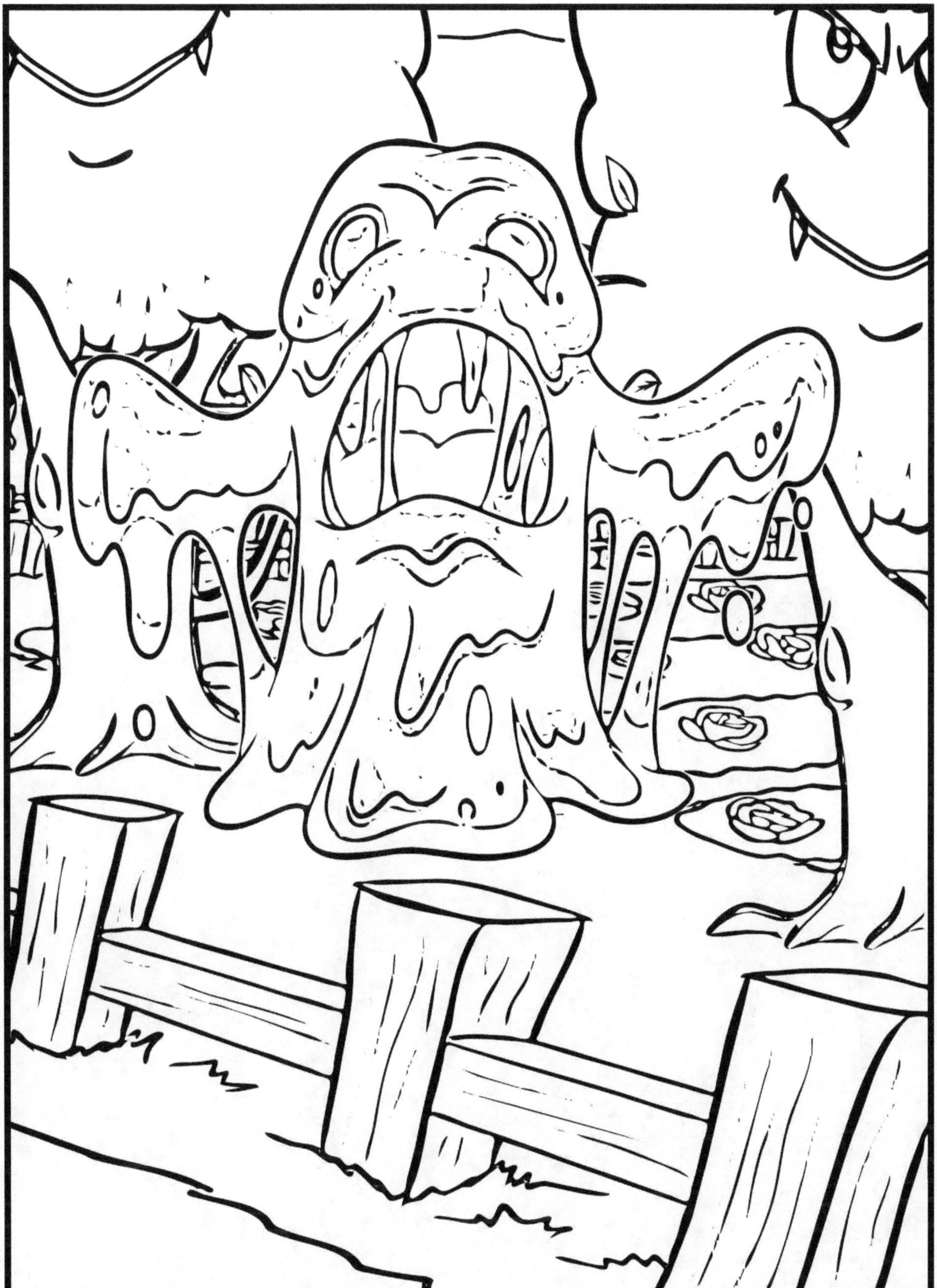

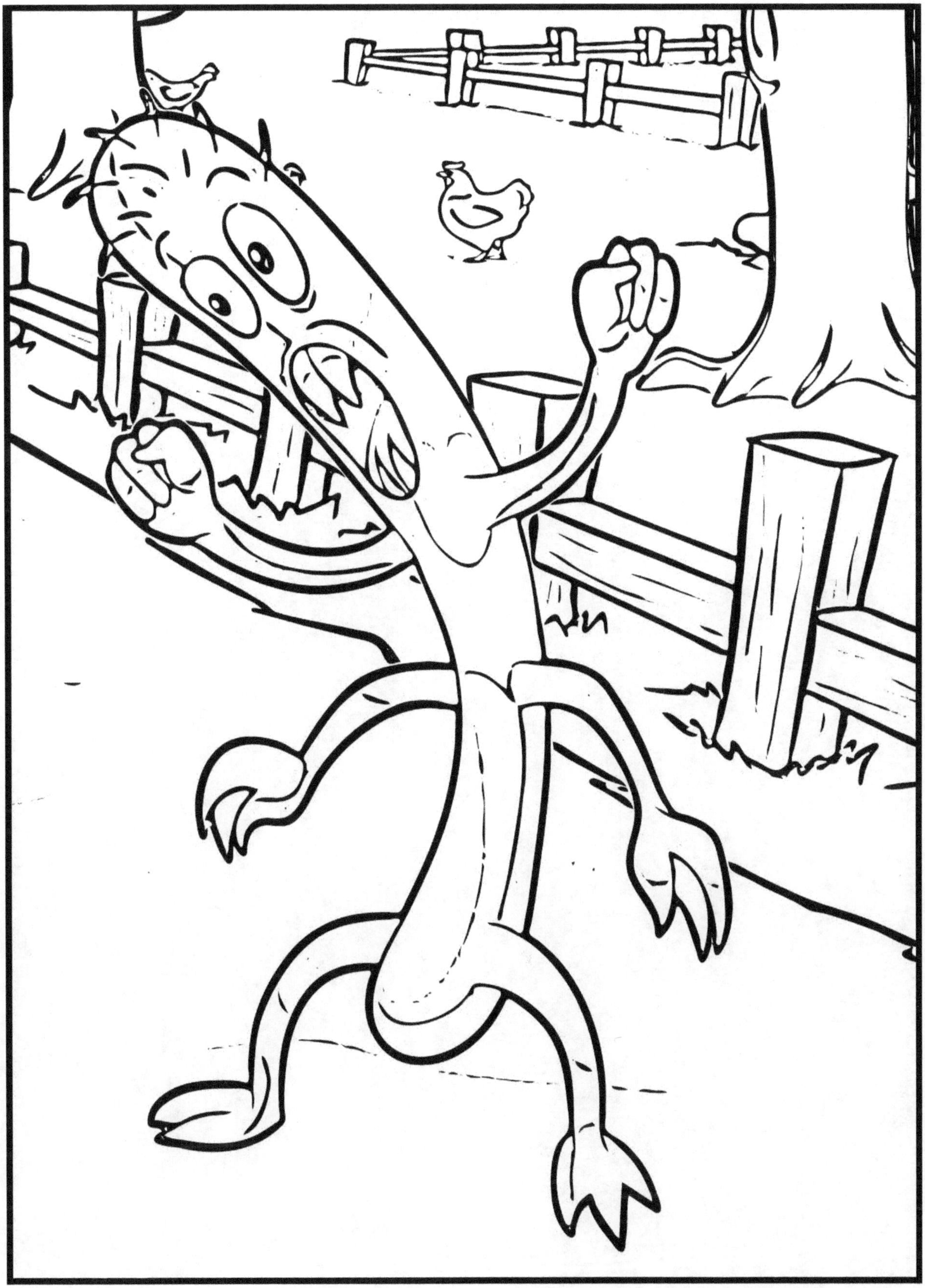

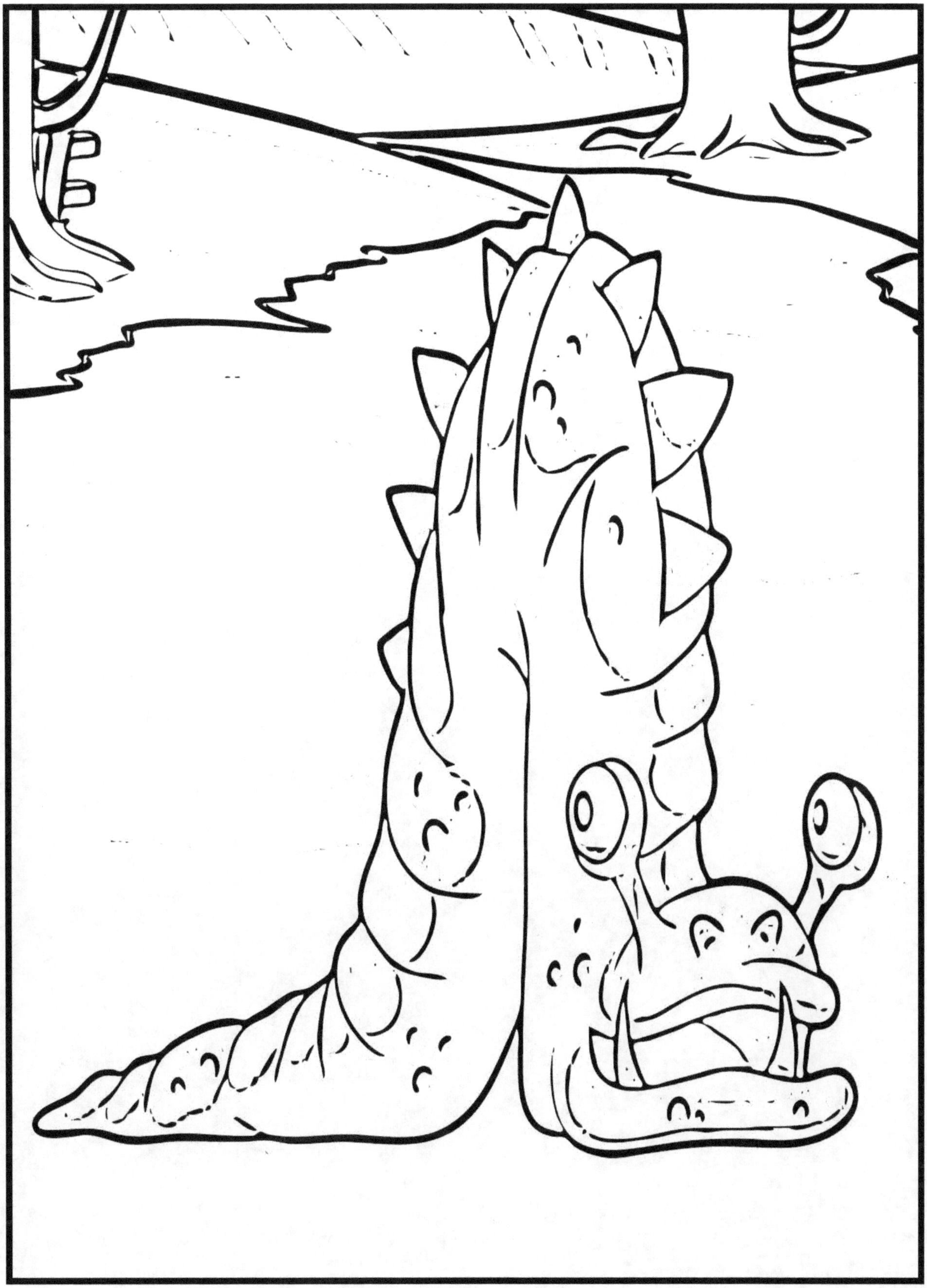

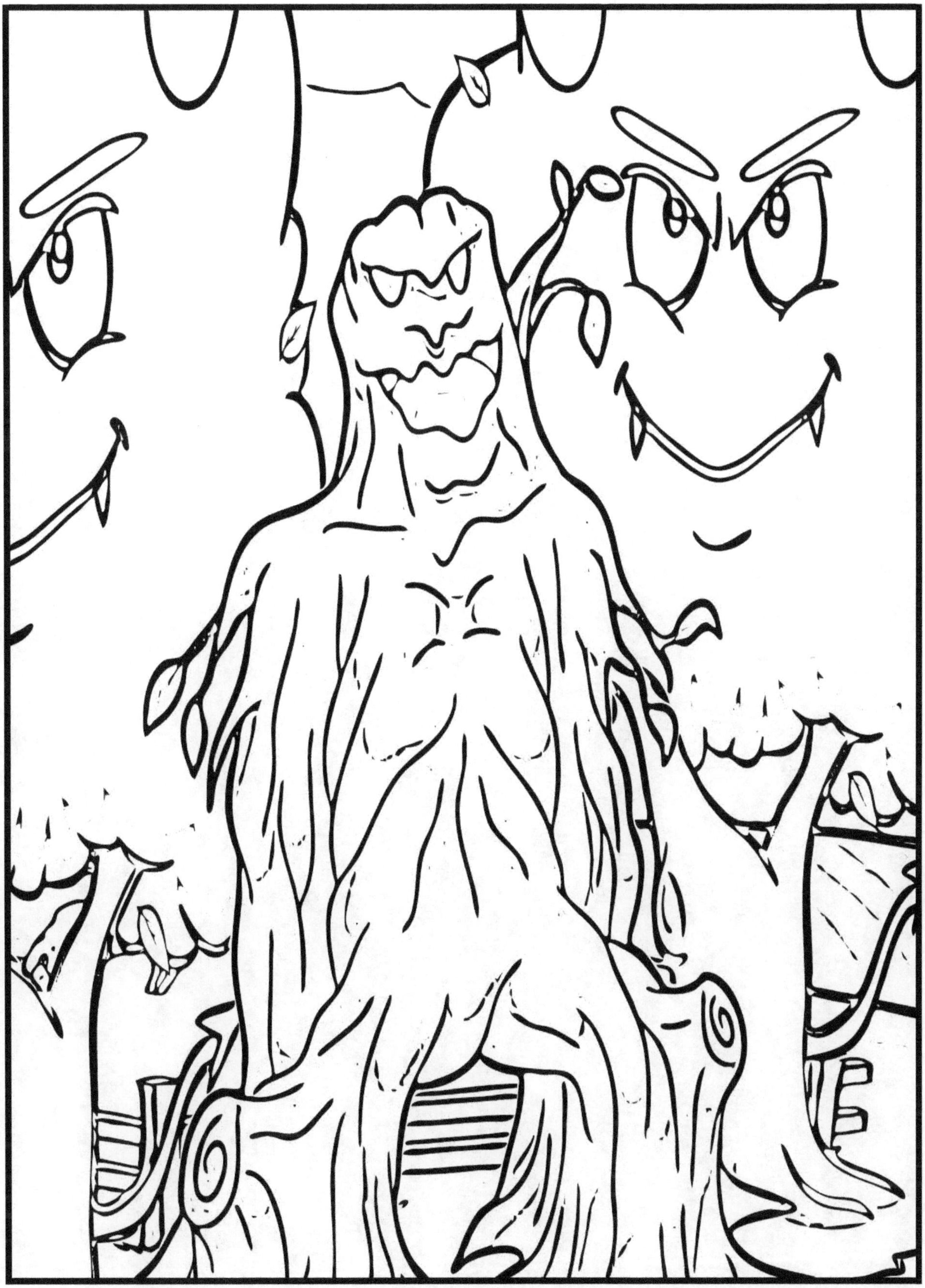

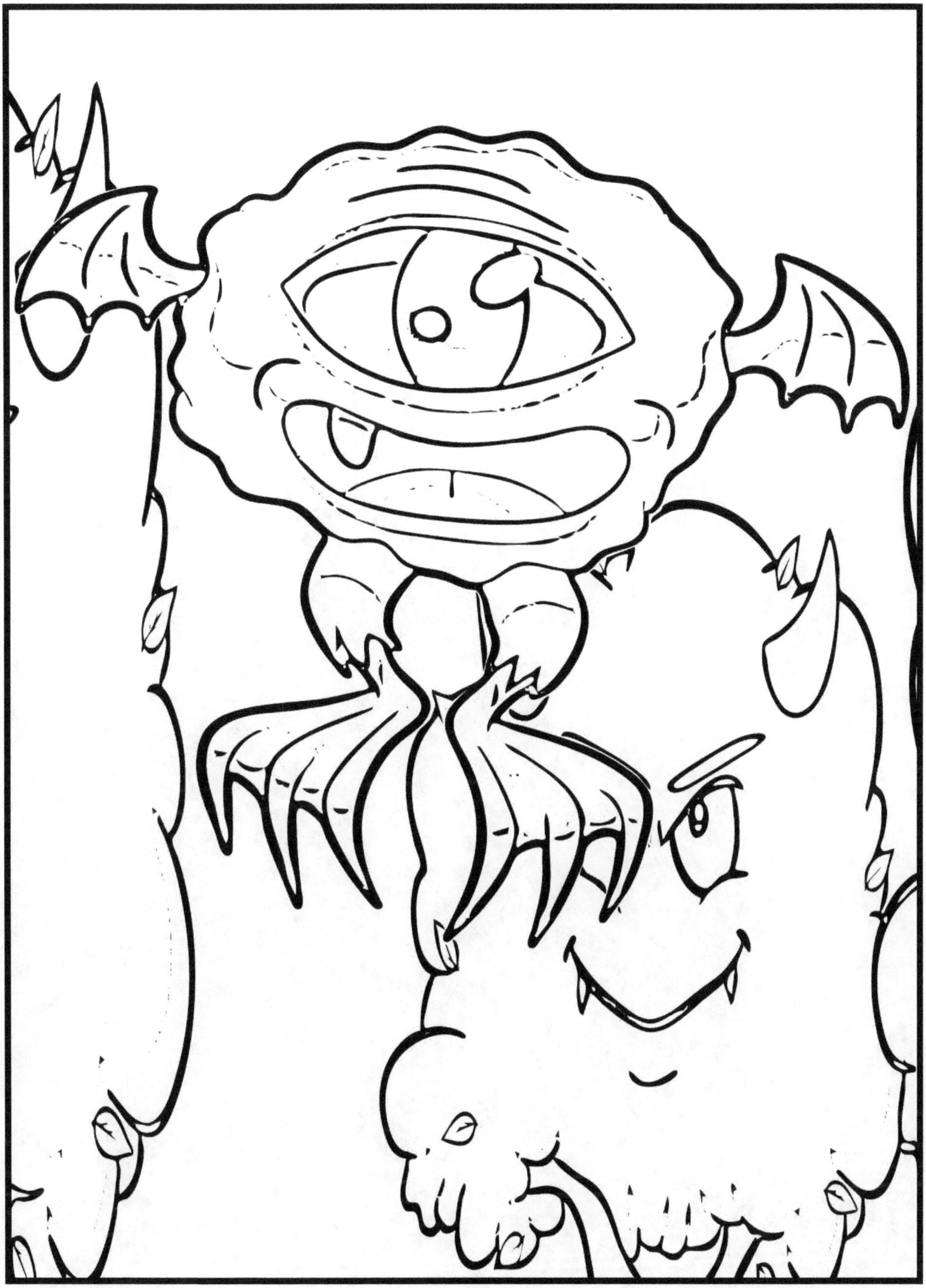

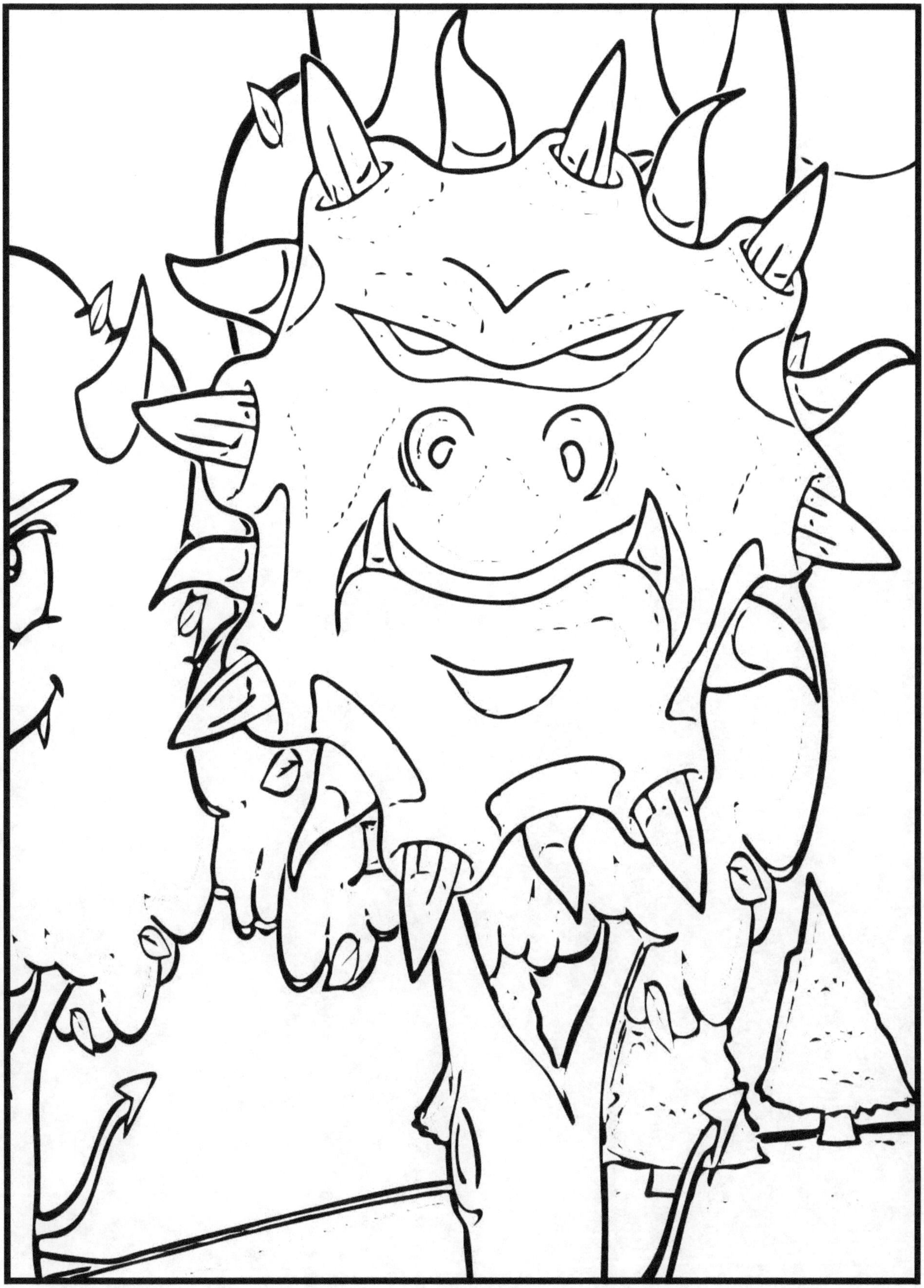

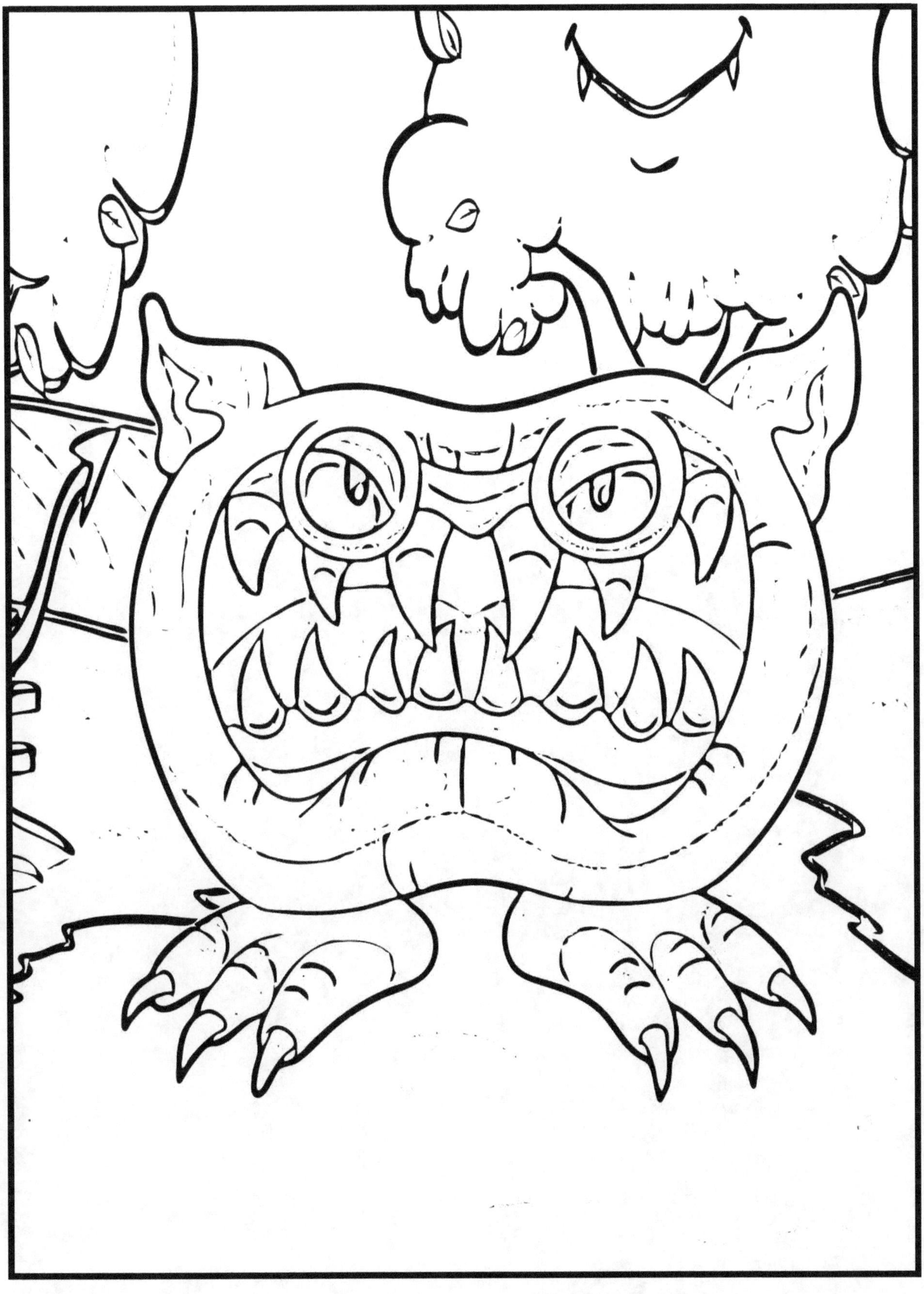

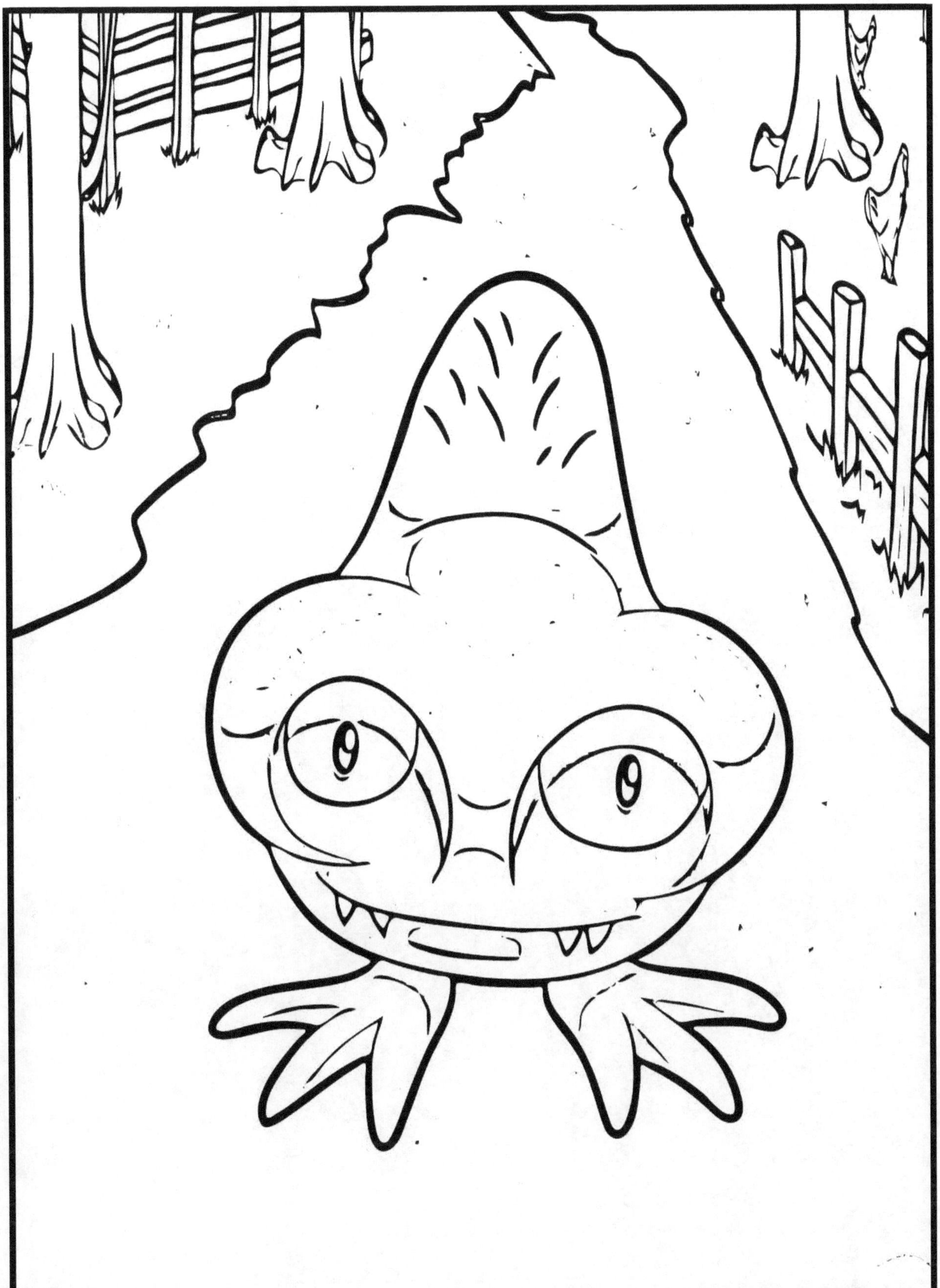

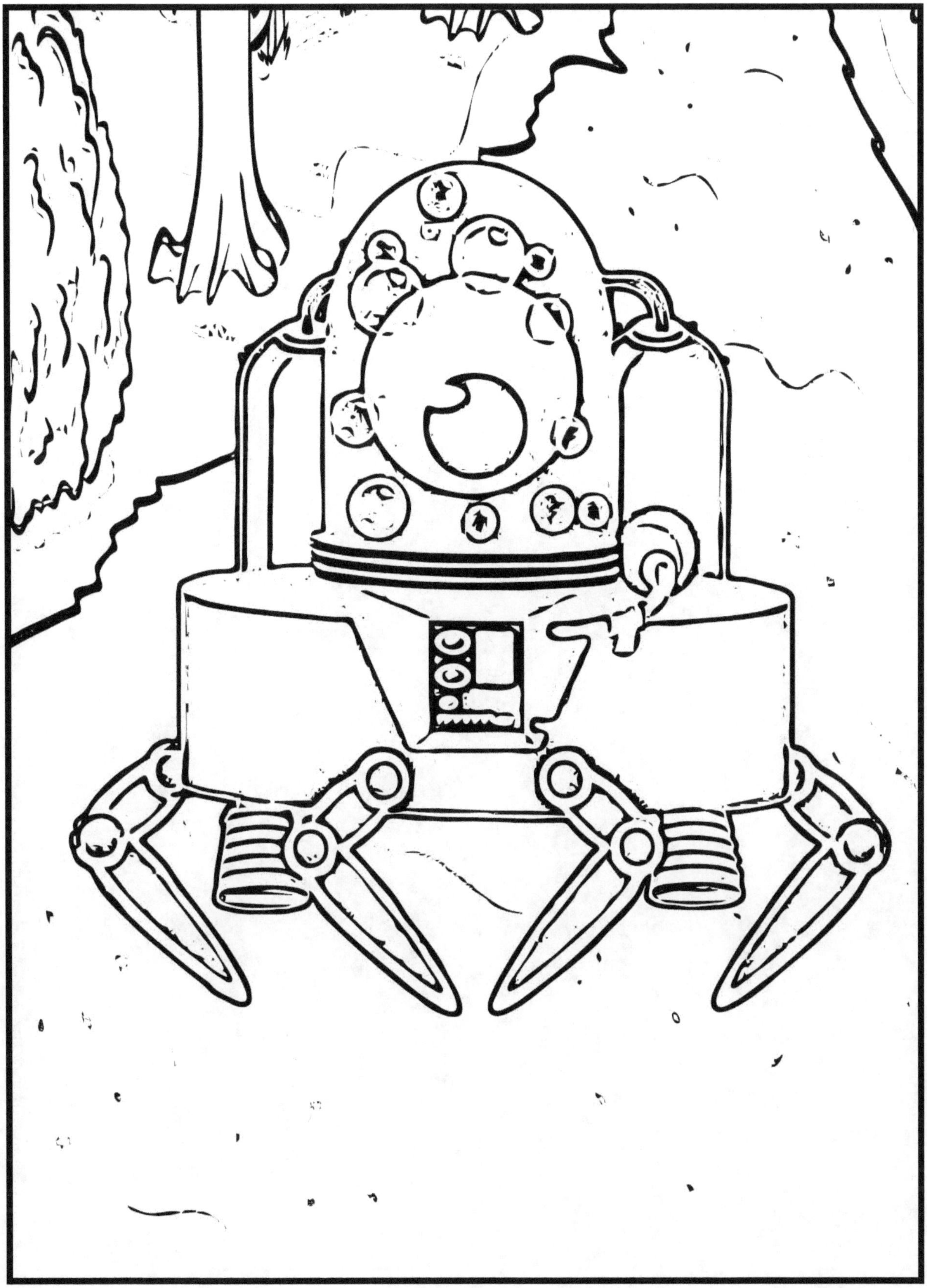

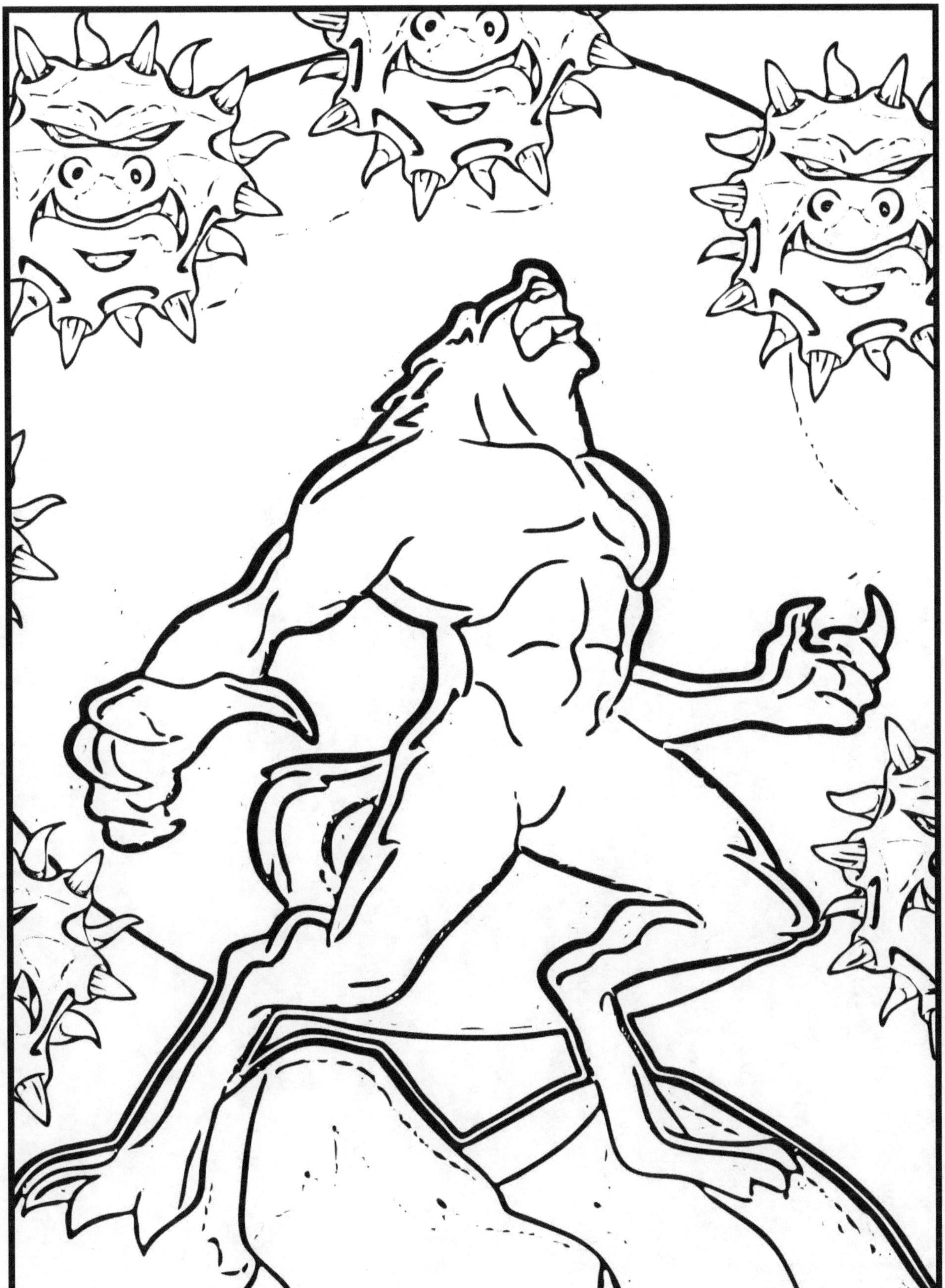

www.ingramcontent.com/pod-product-compliance
Lightning Source LLC
Chambersburg PA
CBHW080618180526
45168CB00007B/2960
* 9 7 8 1 5 1 9 2 0 7 6 5 4 *